Girl, Bye!

RIA RAI HARRIS

Girl, Bye!

10 LIES WOMEN THINK AND TELL THEMSELVES ABOUT MEN

RIA RAI HARRIS

publish your gift

GIRL, BYE!
Copyright © 2023 Ria Rai Harris
All rights reserved.
Published by Publish Your Gift®
An imprint of Purposely Created Publishing Group, LLC

No part of this book may be reproduced, distributed or transmitted in any form by any means, graphic, electronic, or mechanical, including photocopy, recording, taping, or by any information storage or retrieval system, without permission in writing from the publisher, except in the case of reprints in the context of reviews, quotes, or references.

Printed in the United States of America
ISBN: 978-1-64484-622-3 (print)
ISBN: 978-1-64484-623-0 (ebook)

Special discounts are available on bulk quantity purchases by book clubs, associations and special interest groups.
For details email: sales@publishyourgift.com
or call (888) 949-6228.
For information log on to www.PublishYourGift.com

TABLE OF CONTENTS

Introduction 1

Lie #1
If I Look a Particular Way, the Right Man
Will Fall in Love With Me 5

Lie #2
The Platinum Pussy Package Will Attract
and Keep the Right Man 19

Lie #3
"I Don't Care About Your Other Girls.
Just be Good to Me." 27

Lie #4
We Live Together, So He's My Man 39

Lie #5
We've Been Together for Years,
So When He is Ready for Marriage,
I'll Be His Wife 49

Lie #6
The Two of Us Have a Baby, So He's Going to Stay with Me 59

Lie #7
  Having His Baby Gives Me a Real Title with Rights 67

Lie #8
  He Didn't Mean It 75

Lie #9
  If I Love Him Enough, He Will Change ... 91

Lie #10
  It's Okay to Be Called a Bitch 97

Conclusion 103
Acknowledgments 105
About the Author 107

INTRODUCTION

When I initially thought about writing a book, the first topic that came to mind was my life as a Cook County Adult Probation Officer. I spent all of my adult life in that role until I retired after almost thirty-two years. I figured I knew that story like the back of my hand. But, when I assessed who I was writing for, I changed my mind and chose to write a book geared towards women and how some of us think.

I reflected on some of the mistakes I'd made due to my mindset and determined that my debut book would speak to women, young and old, about mistakes we have made and (hopefully for some) ones we can avoid. The choice to delve into some uncomfortable topics was intentional because we cannot fix what we will not face. But, as long as you have breath, you can learn from your past errors in judgment and do better. It's easy for a woman's emotions to cloud her discernment, and I want you to recognize the game before you get played.

At the onset, this book might seem to be about the relationships between men and women, but it isn't. This book is about how women think about themselves regarding *something that is very important to them*—their relationship with men.

I am not a relationship coach; I am a mindset coach. My goal with this book is to show some of the thought processes in which we as women engage and present you with another way to operate. I want you to think about why you're accepting behaviors with which you don't agree just to stay in a relationship with a man. I want you to ask yourself about your frame of mind when you acted in a certain manner. I want you to have a conversation with yourself about how you feel about *you*. And if you don't like where that conversation leads, get help with feeling better about yourself.

This book is not a man bashing tome. I have some wonderful friends that are men, and I would never attack their character. I also know some men that are serial adulterers, domestic abusers, liars, and predators. The only men that should have a problem with what I have written within these pages are those that are engaged in some of those identified problematic behaviors. A hit dog will holler.

Hopefully something that you read in this book will resonate and, when one of the situations and the mentality that accompanies it rears its head, an alarm will go off and tell you to step back, remove the rose-colored glasses, and truly assess what you're about to sign up for. Prayerfully, you (or someone you know) will be spared from having to buy a lesson and, instead, borrow one from the following chapters.

Get ready to hear some lies, see some truths, and experience some *Girl, Bye!* moments.

Buckle up for the roller coaster ride!

LIE #1

IF I LOOK A PARTICULAR WAY, THE RIGHT MAN WILL FALL IN LOVE WITH ME

When I get up in the morning, I see all the imperfections in my face and body. They may be considered small or insignificant to others, but they are huge to me. I agonize over my waistline, which has expanded over the years. I lament over my uneven eyebrows and my lack of long, luscious eyelashes. I scowl at the fat that has taken residence under my chin. And the list goes on and on and on.

Some of my attributes that I really think are attractive, like my full lips and bushy hair, do not necessarily measure up to this society's standards of beauty. I am fairly certain that I am not the only woman in the world that performs this daily personal overview. The next thing I do is fret over what I can do to "fix" some of these qualities that I do not care for when I look in the mirror.

For me, "fixing" is typically using an eyebrow pencil to shape my brows and occasionally getting some lashes applied (for special events). I do what I can for some of the other items on my list of flaws, like wear clothing that camouflages my midsection, and opt to ignore the rest. In this world dominated by optics, women want to be viewed as beautiful and desirable more than ever. So, we look for solutions to the problems that make us look less than perfect.

Do you have excessive facial hair? Your esthetician can wax that right off or, if you have the funds, electrolysis sessions will do the trick. Do you think your nose is too broad? Learning to apply contouring makeup is a must or, if you are really serious about not liking your nose, rhinoplasty is a choice. Do you think your cleavage is too small? If a push up bra isn't enough, budget for breast augmentation. Are you convinced that you need a Brazilian Butt Lift (BBL)? Take a vacation to an island and let the destination also be where you go for getting gluteoplasty and liposuction or, if you're on a budget, go to a hotel suite and pray that the unlicensed person giving you the injections is not shooting something in your body that will harm or kill you. These are just a few of the complaints women that I know have had about themselves and the lengths some of them have been willing to go to correct them. In no way do I endorse any of the aforementioned procedures. I only mention them to enlighten those that are not familiar with some of the body augmentation practices being used today.

Once we decide something about ourselves needs fixing, some of us will move Heaven and Earth to remedy that problem. Did you decide that something about you needs to be changed because you don't like what you see or because others have told you that there are some things about you they don't like? I'm not shaming anyone for how they decide to alter their appearance; my question is about the reason behind the alterations.

A good number of us seek to meet a standard of physical perfection, not just for our own satisfaction but to attract the man of our dreams. We will endanger our health by almost starving ourselves to death because we feel that we're too fat to entice Mr. Right. Often, we put ourselves through changes and procedures, not to improve our physical well-being but to hopefully increase our level of worthiness in men's eyes. We want men to be captivated by our external beauty, like a bee is drawn to a flower's nectar, and we are willing to pay the mental, emotional, physical, and financial price to capture their attention.

One day, my adult son happened to look at my hands. I'd just gotten my nails done and he asked, "Why did you do that?" After figuring out what he was talking about, my answer was, "Because I think they're gorgeous!" He responded, "Well, I hope so because a whole lot of men don't even care about all of that stuff." As he walked away, I thought about a few things:

1. As a young adult man (my son was in his mid-twenties at the time), my son already understood that a lot of beautification that women do is to attract male attention.
2. How many women have shown my son and other men, young and old, that we do so much to our hair, nails, and bodies for the benefit of male attention?

3. Is it possible we don't consciously know that, sometimes, we choose a look we don't like solely because we observe that it attracts men?
4. How much time, effort, and money have I spent (and have other women spent) on enhancements that men didn't care about?

Ladies, ask yourselves this: "If I didn't think that wearing this hairstyle, losing weight, or whatever it is I'm doing to increase my desirability was appealing to men, would I still do it, wear it, or have it simply because I like it?" There is nothing wrong with enhancing your appearance. The question is: for whom are you doing those enhancements? There is definitely a level of attraction that people have for different physical traits, but there is so much more to each of us besides our exterior.

Do you want to be in a relationship with someone that is only interested in you based on your outer shell? What will happen if the physical attribute to which he is so enamored changes? Will he like you less if you gain ten pounds? Is your natural hair a turn-off for him?

If his only concern is that you look magazine cover perfect, does he even really like or know the real you? Many of us are beautiful, but we question our worth because society, as well as specific individuals, feels that our loveliness (that we should be able to determine for ourselves and bring to the table) is not lovely enough.

It is bad enough that social media—and before that music videos, television, movies, and magazines—has shaped the world's view regarding which physical features make women attractive. It is even worse that some of us have bought into this ideology hook, line, and sinker. I am a little (or a lot) older than some of you reading this book. When I was young, I wanted to be a *JET* magazine centerfold because I believed that all of those women were shapely and gorgeous.

My dream was to be a "brick house" with measurements of 36-24-36. Subconsciously, at the age of eight or nine years old, I already knew that those ladies were the crème de la crème in my culture. Why would they be in the magazine wearing that sexy swimwear if they weren't considered beautiful? When I was a teenager, music videos hit the scene and those took what the world considered beautiful to an entirely different level. Having straight, wavy, or curly hair down to the middle of your back, a runway model's figure, and a smooth complexion (the lighter, the better) were the standards placed in front of the masses through music videos.

Genetics are uncontrollable and there should not be any anger or jealousy directed towards the women that were born fitting that description of beauty. The issue was (and is) that the media made a lot of us feel that if you didn't fit into those narrow parameters, you were a less attractive and less desirable ugly duckling. No one wants to be considered unappealing, so some women resorted to wearing wigs and weaves, and using fade creams and waist trainers to abate that feeling of being Cinderella's stepsister or being the bridesmaid but never the bride.

Even in 2023, women are still bound by what others deem attractive. There are women who love wearing their hair in dreadlocks, but because this style is considered unacceptable, unattractive, and even unhygienic by some, many of those ladies either decided to not style their hair in that fashion or changed from that style to please others. How many women have used colored contacts, not because changing their appearance is something fun to do but because a guy she's attracted to likes women with hazel eyes and her natural eye color is brown?

When I look at my reflection, I think about weight loss as a way to get healthier, live longer, and look better in my clothes. But I remember being younger and hearing ladies' conversations about losing weight because some dude said that he didn't date girls that were bigger than a size eight and the woman who was interested in him was a size twelve. There is nothing wrong with wanting to be a size eight; I just want you to become an eight because *you* want that for yourself, not to impress someone else. If you like yourself as a size twelve, *please* do not become an eight because you're hoping there is a possibility that you'll get asked out by that guy because you now meet his size requirement.

TRUTH #1:

Your looks alone do not guarantee that you will attract the right man who will fall in love with you and the two of you will live happily ever after.

No matter how well put together you are, how beautiful your skin is, how perfectly arched your eyebrows are, how manicured your fingers and toes are, and how gorgeous your hair flows, most men will sense if you are operating from a place of desperation. When you are so intent on having a man, the wolves will smell your unhappiness with being single even if it's covered by fashionable clothing and expertly applied makeup. The average man can perceive a woman's insecurities and, if he's the predatory type, he will approach you with flowery comments and smooth conversation. He will use all the correct verbiage to make you feel good about yourself. There are a couple of problems with this scenario.

The first issue is your insecurities attracting the wrong man. Predatory men will say and do anything they can to make you feel like you're on top of the world. Typically, once they get you hooked, they flip the script on you so you'll feel that you can't leave them because no one else will want you (according to the predator). I'll discuss this problem in more detail in a later chapter.

You may encounter men that engage in gaslighting, which is "manipulating someone, using psychological methods, into questioning their own sanity or powers of reasoning" according to Dictionary.com. He lures you in with his charm, then slowly says and does things to diminish your self-confidence, which is even easier to do if you're already insecure.

In the old movie, *Gaslight*, the husband does things to make the wife question if she's losing her mind. He literally started with small changes, like moving objects in their home, and pretended that he didn't know what she was talking about when she asked about the items not being in their original place. I won't spoil it and reveal the ending of the movie but know this—the man the main character falls in love with turns out to be her tormenter. Being gaslighted can have you question your ability to make sound choices and, instead of trusting yourself, cause you to turn over decision-making power to a man whose intentions towards you are malevolent. This type of man is a true predator that looks for women he can exploit.

Narcissistic men seek women that will cosign their projected view of themselves. Who better to find for the job of gassing up a truly insecure man than a woman that is wrestling with her own insecurities? The narcissist requires your constant admiration and makes it seem like he deserves to be first and foremost in everyone's reality, particularly the woman that he's chosen to grace with his presence. The truth of the matter is he's a weak, apprehensive man who embellishes what little accomplishments he's achieved (if any), seeks to convince you that he's always right, has no consideration for others' feelings (especially his wife or woman), and actually needs a woman to prop him up.

This is the man that will denigrate you in public by correcting your perceived mistakes and shining light on what he feels are your shortcomings, but he cannot tolerate being treated the same way. This man wants people to think he knows so much about everything but, in actuality, he is a bully that is hiding his deficits. This coward is another type of predator to be wary of.

The second issue is that you haven't gotten to the point where you feel good about yourself without someone else having to cosign. Until you love the skin you're in, I don't advise that you get involved in a relationship. In 2010, I took a two-year sabbatical from dating to adjust my mental state. I had spent so much time working on relationships instead of working on myself that I'd lost touch with who I was, what I wanted out of life, and the route I would take to obtain my desires. Once I spent time getting to know myself again, establishing my goals and working towards accomplishing them, I then took the time to determine what type of man and relationship I wanted. My previous relationship faux pas taught me that I needed to get straight with God and be happy with myself first, know what I wanted in a partner and from that union, and not settle for less.

Although hearing compliments is wonderful, you should not depend on someone else's words and deeds to define your self-worth. If you are in a relationship, the gentleman should say and do things to make you happy and *reinforce* what you feel about yourself. His adoration is the candles, but your love of self is the cake as well as the icing on it. Conversely, his not saying or doing the things that initially attracted you to him are cause for a conversation and should make you unhappy with him, perhaps, but not unhappy with yourself. Even if a man isn't exploitive yet your looks attracted him, external beauty alone will not keep him.

How many women that are considered *gorgeous* have had their significant others cheat on them? There are too many to count, but I can list Halle Berry, Janet Jackson, and Nia Long just to name a few. Please don't believe that your having every hair in place guarantees fidelity, monogamy, or love. I still want you to look like, smell like, and *be* the fabulous woman you are when you show up in the world. Just do not think that doing so will create a covenant between you and the man of your dreams.

TAKEAWAY

1. All of us are imperfect and have things about us that we would like to change.
2. No matter how perfect you look, that will not guarantee that a man will treat you how you deserve to be treated.
3. Predators are lurking and ready to take advantage of your insecurities. Don't let them.
4. Please don't tell me that you spent your rent money on a lace front, lashes, a manicure or pedicure, and a Brazilian to impress a dude that works part time at the car wash! *Girl, Bye!* Seriously, nothing is wrong with enhancing your physical appearance as long as you are doing so to please yourself, not someone else.

THE PLATINUM PUSSY PACKAGE WILL ATTRACT AND KEEP THE RIGHT MAN

Many years ago, I discovered that some women thought they had a Platinum Pussy Package, which they could use to get and keep a man. I am defining The Platinum Pussy Package as a vagina that is always considered "tight and wet" no matter the number of sexual encounters and can damn near do tricks (like smoke a cigarette). Throw in some ass clapping, a little private pole dancing, a personal lap dance, and *voila*! You have a Platinum Pussy Package!

If you decide to have a sexual relationship with a man, I am all for your having The Package. Just don't be of the opinion that said Package guarantees that a man will be loyal to you. The Package can't even guarantee that a man even likes you. He may love The Package but not care about the rest of you. Some men will have sex with you on a regular basis and may even take you out every now and then, but they will not accept the title of "your man," regardless to how good your Package makes them feel.

Many lifetimes ago, I worked with a spoken word artist that held shows and events. At one particular pre-Valentine's Day event in Chicago, my best friend and I worked the door as well as handled the set-up and break down for the show. We did a lot of circulating from the entrance to the back of the venue. The event was held on a cold February evening but still drew a packed house. Both of us were stunned into silence when, on one of our trips to check on something before the show started, we noticed a young woman on the front row wearing an extremely short mini-dress and no stockings, sitting with her legs open. She didn't have on any panties!

Anyone that is familiar with Chicago's weather knows that February is glacial, even more so at night. If the two of us saw her personal pocketbook (another term I use for vagina) while casually walking by and glancing in her direction, then the artists that performed that night had the opportunity to see her entire

Package if she chose to leave her legs open. So could anyone else that walked past her and looked her way. I do not know which artist she wanted to take notice of her after show delights, but she definitely had someone in mind.

That memory made me consider a couple of things:

1. If some women are operating like this to attract the attention of men on what I consider to be a small time, local stage, I can't imagine what packages, pocketbooks, and delights are being offered to well-known artists, athletes, politicians, and pastors.

2. I question the modus operandi of anyone who wants to be more than an overnight sensation but is willing to bear the frozen tundra that is Chicago on a February night wearing nothing but a coat, a tiny dress, bra, and shoes in the hopes of enticing someone with their exposed vagina.

Some women think their Platinum Pussy Package is strong enough to "take somebody's man."

I take umbrage to a few points based on this mentality:

1. There should be no pride in "taking" a man. You have then become a party to the breaking up of a relationship and potentially a home (though the overwhelming responsibility for that would fall on the man).
2. You cannot "take" a man from a woman; he either chooses you or he chooses her.
3. Your Platinum Pussy Package isn't the only one in existence and there is at least one woman in your man's neighborhood that has a deeper, tighter, wetter Platinum Pussy Package than yours.
4. There are very few Platinum Pussy Packages that can clap and snap at the same fabulous level for decades. Some women forget that after having a few babies and many penises, your Platinum gets downgraded to Silver, and that man you were so proud to "steal" will be stolen by a new and improved Platinum Pussy Package.

Just like you used yours to "take" someone's man, be confident in the fact that someone new will use theirs to "take" this same man from you. If all he is about is the joys of your Package, the person offering him the Package is interchangeable. I was once in a relationship with a man that some felt was "stolen" by another woman who used everything she could, including her Package, to get his attention. The woman was familiar to me and had actually attempted to "befriend" me. My response was that he could not be stolen as he was not a possession; he was a man that made a choice. At the end of the day, I was grateful to her for exposing who he was, who she was, and for sparing me from spending another moment with a man that did not value me. I chose me and my worth over being a part of his stable of women.

TRUTH #2:

Your Platinum Pussy Package alone
will not get you more than a wet ass.

Most men will not take a woman seriously when they feel that she's handing out sex like she would pass out Tic Tac's. A good number of men do "body counts," which is basically inquiring about the number of men with whom a woman has had sex. If you've dealt sexually with too many men or specific men, like guys in their circle, they'll join the lineup for sex but probably won't go any further than that. Men don't want the "get around, good time girl" to be their girlfriend and definitely not their wife.

Ladies, what is your end game? What title do you want to hold? If you are looking for a "no strings attached, I'll see you when I see you" situation, that's fine. You have no expectations for a long-term relationship. But, if you are desirous of becoming a wife, having a clapping, snapping coochie (an old-time term for vagina) is not enough. You have to offer more than your willingness to lay down with a guy at any time and any place. You are more than your vagina.

TAKEAWAY

1. Determine what you want from the man first. Do you want to be his sex partner only or are you looking to be in a long-term relationship?

2. If you're looking for a durable relationship that does not have sex as its foundation, don't offer your Platinum Pussy Package out of the gate. Find out if you really like him and how he treats you first. Build an emotional connection before getting caught up in a sexual entanglement.

3. You are more than your vagina, regardless of how you choose to use it.

4. Please don't tell me that you thought that "taking" someone's man made you the better woman. *Girl, Bye!* Seriously, it just makes you a treacherous one.

LIE #3

"I DON'T CARE ABOUT YOUR OTHER GIRLS. JUST BE GOOD TO ME."

In 1983, The S.O.S. Band released the song "Just Be Good To Me." I was in high school at the time, and I clearly remember singing the hook, "People always talking about your reputation. I don't care about your other girls. Just be good to me." In my mind, it was just a song that I liked because I enjoyed the music the group made. At that time, I didn't realize that some women were really operating with that mentality.

Note: If you are voluntarily in a polygamous relationship, I respect your decision. You are engaged in a lifestyle where everyone knows all of the involved parties, and everyone agrees to respect the boundaries of said relationship. This life choice is not for me, but I take no issue with others living a life of their choosing, even when it's one I don't choose for myself.

For those of you that are casually dating, the expectation should be that the gentleman is seeing other women and you should be able to date other men if you so choose. You aren't at the point where exclusivity is on the table, so this lie doesn't necessarily include you.

Nonetheless, please continue reading for future reference. When you are in a relationship that has progressed past the initial dating phase, there should be a different level of expectation that you discuss with the gentleman. Hopefully, you and he are on the same page. But, if he tells you that you're still one of two or more (or lies and says you're the only one but you have proof that he's still seeing other women), you have a decision to make. If you truly aren't interested in polygamy but find yourself accepting or ignoring the fact that your "man" is a lot of women's "man," you've given him permission to continue being in multiple relationships. You've decided that you would rather have a piece of a man since you're sharing him with others (and that isn't your desire) instead of not being in a relationship until you meet a man that will be faithful to you. Let's discuss being a girlfriend that shares her "man," a mistress, and a wife that knows her husband is unfaithful.

As a girlfriend, you have limited rights because the man has no legal obligation to you. All you have is what he agrees to. If he says he's going to be monogamous on all levels (physically, mentally emotionally, financially, and spiritually), hopefully he's telling the truth. But, if he isn't, it's up to you to determine your worth as well as how you are going to handle the situation. You can give him another chance to see if he is going to change and be monogamous, you can let the relationship go, or you can share him.

Whatever you choose is up to you. All I ask is that you are true to yourself and do what is in your best interest because I don't see him putting your interest before his. If you decide to ignore his having other women, that's fine. Please don't get angry down the road if the relationship doesn't work out how you planned; you chose this. But, if at any point you decide this situation is not for you and it is not meeting your needs, leave in peace. There's no need for drama, fighting, or falling out. In the words of "Blame It On Me" by Chrisette Michele let him "say anything that you want as long as it's over." He will be just fine. And so will you.

I have a few associates that have been mistresses. The women were clear about the fact that their "man" was legally married to another woman and chose to enter a romantic relationship with him anyway. For whatever reason, these women chose to be a part of a triangle instead of being solo. They typically had their own holidays; Valentine's Day was February 15 because he had to spend February 14 with his wife. Christmas gifts would be exchanged on December 26 because December 25 was reserved for his family.

Whatever the mistress planned for his birthday had to be scheduled around the time that his wife celebrated his birthday as he would not blow her off to be with his side chick. Depending on the situation, he could not accompany her to social outings where they'd look like a couple because her "man" couldn't risk being seen by someone that would tell his wife. The reasons a man (better known as someone else's husband) seeks a relationship outside of his marriage are many; for instance, "my wife and I have grown apart," "I don't want my children to come from a broken home," and "my wife punishes me by withholding sex or affection." Is his personal anthem "She's Got Papers On Me" by Richard "Dimples" Fields? Let's assume that the reason someone else's husband gives to explain why he doesn't want to be with his wife anymore and wants to be with you, the potential mistress, is the one hundred percent truth. Then there are a couple of options for him—*stay married or get divorced*! It's just that simple. Ladies, why downgrade yourselves to play the role of understudy for a lead role that you, more than likely, will never get to play. Not many mistresses become the wives of the man to whom they were formerly a paramour. Those that do spend a lot of time watching for signs that her now-husband isn't looking for a newer, younger model to fill the space that she vacated.

Let's be clear about another point. If, God forbid, something unfortunate befalls the man, his wife is the person that is acknowledged, not the mistress. Pension benefits, social security disbursements, property, and other assets typically go to his wife and their children. If the mistress has children with someone else's husband and no special provisions are made for her or the children (such as insurance policies and property being bought in her name only), there is a good chance that she and those children will be left in the cold. If the place the mistress stays in is owned by someone else's husband and he dies, I cannot imagine his widow being so compassionate that she would let the mistress continue to live there. Now the mistress is not only grieving, she's also facing homelessness.

Even if I didn't care about obtaining anything for myself, I would want my children provided for as they are innocent and deserve that much. For the mistresses that don't care about not being financially provided for by someone to whom they've given their time and a portion of their lives, that is fine. I would hope that you'd want to be left with a little more that memories, but that's me.

Note: Being separated is *still being married*. A person is either single, married, divorced, or widowed. Period.

If you're the wife and know that there is another woman (or women) in a relationship with your husband, what is your reason for staying? To keep your family intact? Finances? Are you too embarrassed to let others know that your marriage is failing? There's pee in the dating pool so you don't want to get in the water? Are you singing "He's Mine" by MoKenStef to convince yourself that it's better to be your husband's number one, knowing that there is a number two, than to be without him at all? Whatever the reason, be sure it's worth your self-respect. I know some women in this position and a few of them have resorted to low-key competing with the mistress, hoping that the best woman wins, and that she (the wife) will be the best woman. If your husband has put you in the position to defend your title, you've already lost.

One wife I know took the competition to an unfathomable level. She knew her husband's mistress; they lived in the same community and attended the same church. Every time the mistress got pregnant, the wife got pregnant soon after and vice versa. The two of them each brought four babies into the world in this battle royale for a total of eight human beings. This amazed me because I'm convinced that the man over which they competed for a couple of decades isn't worth all of this smoke and they literally gave birth to people, partially because of this long-standing skirmish. This is an extreme example but, sadly, a real one.

TRUTH #3:

Many women's first choice is to not be a part of a man's harem and *they do* care about the existence of other women as it relates to their spouse or husband, but they will choose this option over being single.

You can be number one, number two, or number ten in a man's rotation. As long as your only concern is his treatment of you when he's with you, you are not a victim of his shenanigans; you are a volunteer. Too often, we as women do not accept our responsibility for being in certain situations. It's so easy to make the man a villain and for us to play the role of victim when he is dating multiple women. But, once you know, you have the choice to stay or leave. If you choose to remain as a part of his stable, you have consciously decided that being with this man is more important to you than your values and the lifestyle you told yourself you want. The fear of being single and alone supersedes your desire to be in a monogamous relationship. Until you are willing to uphold your standards, do not expect him to respect your boundaries, your desires, or you.

TAKEAWAY

1. Write a list of your personal beliefs as well as your desires regarding your intimate relationships (i.e., I expect to be in a trusting, loving, monogamous relationship). Then compare what is on your list to the relationship you're currently in. If there are significant differences between your list of beliefs and desires versus your present-day liaison, think deeply about the reason you've chosen to be in a situation that does not align with your wants, needs, and expectations.

2. Choose to have a conversation with your significant other about the parts of your relationship that are not symmetrical with your wants and needs. Decide how you will proceed after having that discussion. If he agrees that your desires are valid and he's willing to work towards providing them, great! If what you seek is more than he can give, you have a decision to make. You can peacefully leave this situation or continue to stay in an entanglement that leaves you

lacking. Either way, you are responsible for choosing the coupling you're in. You have the option to leave this interlude that does not fulfill your wants and the power to walk away from a man that gives you less than you deserve. The decision is yours.

3. If this man is not interested in having the same level of love as you do, be willing to wait for the man that offers you the relationship that you seek. Or, be prepared to stay in a cycle of settling, being disappointed, and having second-class status with the man you chose to stay with.

4. Please don't tell me that you respect yourself while you stay with this bum ass dude that's playing you and all of his other concubines. *Girl, Bye!* Seriously, when you settle for what he's willing to give instead of what you really want, that's fine. Just don't complain about what he's doing to you because he isn't doing anything to you. You're the one playing yourself short, so own it.

LIE #4

WE LIVE TOGETHER, SO HE'S MY MAN

Have you thought about the possibility that how you perceive things is not the way someone else does, especially when it comes to relationships? Oftentimes, women operate from their emotions and let those feelings dictate their reality instead of getting confirmation from the other person in the situation. By confirmation I mean sitting down with the gentleman you're seeing and asking him about the status of your relationship, or even if this is a relationship. If you assume instead of confirming, you're setting yourself up for a tremendous amount of hurt.

To a lot of women, it makes sense that when you and a man decide to live together and he isn't your relative or platonic friend, you and he are in a committed relationship. I beg to differ. If the conversation about his moving in with you, your moving in with him, or the two of you moving somewhere together does not include the discussion about the direction and title of the relationship once you take that step, you may not be happy with what you find out regarding his viewpoint later.

Many years ago, I knew a young woman who was living with a gentleman. She was in the throes of planning the wedding extraordinaire! She had already selected the wedding's theme, she had chosen the design for her wedding dress and the bridesmaids' outfits, and she had selected the location for their nuptials. Her train of thought was that they had dated, now they were living together, and next they would become husband and wife. I knew her "man" and, when I saw him again, I congratulated him on the pending marriage.

He told me that he wasn't getting married. Confused, I asked if he lived with the young lady, and he confirmed that he did. Even more confused, I asked if she was his girlfriend and he said she was not. His explanation was that he never told her that she was his girlfriend so if that is what she assumed that was her fault. That reasoning was both a shocker and an eye opener for me. Our conversation quickly made me get really clear about the value of communication.

Lie #4

According to Dictionary.com, a roommate is "a person occupying the same apartment or house as another." The man I spoke of in the previous paragraph felt free to describe himself as the woman's roommate with whom he also had sex. But, because there were no spoken and established boundaries or confirmation about the nature of the relationship, he was able to play the game of "you can't hold me to something I didn't say or agree to." There are men and women that live together; she thinks they're in a relationship while he's telling people that she is his roommate.

Too often, a woman chooses to not communicate her wants and needs to a man because she's afraid of the man's response (which should be a red flag). So many women are worried that if they ask a man about the nature of their relationship, they'll be told that he sees them as someone that's cool to hang out with, that the sex is phenomenal, and that he trusts her. But despite all of that, they aren't in a relationship. The concern is that once the guy has said those things, you'll have to decide to either accept a position you don't want or leave a situation when you don't really want to because you like him, maybe even love him, and want to give him time to change his mind and get on board with your view of the relationship. The problem with waiting for this guy to catch up with you and your view of the relationship is that he probably won't. And knowing that he does not love you the way you love him will hurt. Leaving him will be hard because your heart wants something that your head knows you won't get. But staying with him and waiting for him to change, when he probably will not, will hurt even more for much longer. It will also make you bitter, spiteful, and resentful. You'll become someone that you don't like and don't even recognize. Keep your integrity and your peace. Let him go.

TRUTH #4:

When you base your understanding of the relationship on how he treats you, that he's introduced you to his family, *that he lives with you*, and you assume he's your man, that's conjecture. Until he says aloud that he is your man that lives with you, you really have a roommate with whom you chose to have sex.

Lie #4

When you and a man live together and someone asks you if he's your man, what's the real answer? Is he your man, a housemate, a live in sex partner, or some guy that's homeless and you felt sorry for him so you offered him a place to stay? Do you truly know how he would answer if asked the same question? If you are not solid about both his response and yours, you're in a bad position. Your thoughts, wishes, dreams, and desires not equaling his truth will have you hurt down the road because the two of you are in different places emotionally. Your feelings will create expectations of him that he didn't sign up for which isn't fair to him or you.

    I don't expect a couple in their twenties to have the same level of self-awareness and understanding of their relationship's depths, even if they live together, as a couple in their forties. I do expect that both parties are clear about the status of their relationship when living together, regardless to the couple's ages. Being a long-term roommate with sexual benefits or being known as that couple that is so in love but, for some reason, can't make it to the alter aren't goals to which you aspire. If, after living together for a couple of years, you or your guy still aren't ready for marriage then consider the possibility that this man is not supposed to be your husband. Cut your losses and let your housemate go so your husband can find you.

Do not think that I am not holding the man who does this accountable for his part in this charade. It's wrong for him to have sex with you, take you to the family functions, then move in with you but not clearly state the nature of your friendship with sexual benefits, relationship, or whatever he considers it to be. But, if you let him go through time operating like this and you don't address it, you have not lived up to your responsibility to yourself. Clarify your expectations before he shows up on your doorstep with all of his belongings in a garbage bag and an Xbox in his backpack.

Lie #4

TAKEAWAY

1. Too often we either make assumptions about the nature of the relationship we are in, or we are too afraid to ask the man to clarify our standing out of fear that he will say something that we don't like. The adage about assuming is "you make an ass of you and me." When you do not have a clear understanding about your connection to the guy that you want to be your man, you run the risk of being told, "I never promised you that" or "I never said that" and he would be telling the truth.

It's better to be up front about what you're seeking and see if this is a role he wants to fill. You do not have to discuss wedding locations and children's names on the first date, but after establishing that you're vibing with him and want to have a future that includes him, be as sure as you can be that he is in the same emotional space. That can only be done by having true heart to heart conversations and watching to be sure that his actions match what his mouth said.

2. Before my husband and I took our relationship to a sexual level, we talked about the good things in our childhood, the rough patches we had growing up, and why we felt our past relationships had not worked. We got clear about having the same relationship goals. Some uncomfortable truths about our shortcomings were discussed. Those conversations gave us a better chance of our relationship thriving before we became intimate.

3. Do not ignore the spoken or unspoken signs that what he says is not in alignment with how he operates. When I went to a class reunion with my now ex-boyfriend, he was quick to present me to the men as his woman. When he introduced me to the women, I became his "friend" all of a sudden. He was happy to show me off to the men but wanted to keep his options open when it came to the women. Needless to say, that was a spoken sign that the relationship he said we had and that I thought we had was a total lie. I chose to free myself from that illusion and that man soon afterwards.

4. Please don't tell me that you're housing, feeding, and clothing a dude and you don't know if he's your man. *Girl, Bye!* Seriously, do not let a man move in with you without knowing from his mouth if he's a roommate with benefits or if he sees himself as being in an intimate relationship with you, and you both have the same definition of what that intimate relationship is.

WE'VE BEEN TOGETHER FOR YEARS, SO WHEN HE IS READY FOR MARRIAGE, I'LL BE HIS WIFE

How many women do you know that stayed with a man that was seemingly faithful to her, made her a part of almost every aspect of his life, stayed with her for years, then married someone he met less than two years ago? So many women have been committed to, loved, lived with, played the wife role without the title, and had children with men only to find themselves discarded like trash when that man marries a different woman. This experience is horrifying! The feelings of betrayal are unimaginable! My question is, "What did the woman sign up for?"

There is an old adage that says, "Why buy the cow when you can get the milk for free?" It seems so antiquated in these modern times, but there is still some truth to it. If a woman is doing everything that the position demands but doesn't have the job, what is the man's motivation to "upgrade" her status? It's fine to aid the less fortunate, but get past the point in life where you're volunteering your time and energy for what is a paid position. Falling back on a word I use often, did you *communicate* your expectations? Did the conversation about marriage ever come up? What did he say? Some guys will lie and say whatever is necessary to keep you with them in the position they want you to fill, even when they know that's not the position you want long-term. I'm not suggesting you have a rigid, set date by which you must be married. I am saying that time moves quickly, and it is quite possible to look up and ten years have passed with you still being his "woman" when both of you know that your desire is to be his wife.

There are men that will tell you the truth. Some of my male associates have told me that they told their "lady friends" that they did not believe in legal marriage or that they weren't sure what the future held, and the women chose to stay. The common reason I've been told for women staying in this situation is that those women thought the guy would change

Lie #5

his mind. Look at the former Camilla Parker Bowles, now Camilla, Queen Consort of the United Kingdom. After over thirty years of being the backup chick, she now has the man plus a royal title. Because King Charles III had been married previously and they had been in love prior to his first marriage, perhaps she thought that he'd give matrimony another try. But a good number of the men I know that have had a rough first marriage are very reluctant to go down the aisle again. They also are typically carrying a lot of baggage from their prior relationship that they need to address and heal from before entering in a new romance. Single men that have never been married may just want that aforementioned milk without being responsible for the cow. Either way, believe them when they tell you that they are not interested in marriage and govern yourself accordingly.

Early in the dating phase, so many women were told by the man that they were not looking for marriage and decided to stay with the guy, knowing that they wanted to get married. These same women were livid and accused the men of "cheating them out of their youth" and "playing games with them" after the men stuck with their original statement and did not proffer a marriage proposal. In all honesty, the ladies played themselves. When a man tells you his truth (which his actions should verify), believe him. Then make the decision to either stay in the arrangement that isn't what you want with no expectations beyond what the guy said or move on.

There are men that will lie to you about marriage because they enjoy the benefits that they receive from being with you but don't want to obligate themselves to legally marrying YOU. They just want to keep you locked down because, although they may really like you (or at least like what you do for them), they either aren't ready for that level of commitment or they don't love you but don't want you to do for someone else what you do for them. Some of these guys will marry you and your marriage typically turns out to be a complete shit show because that isn't what he really wanted to do. Other men will give you the engagement ring and, five years later, you're still his fiancée.

It does not take five or more years to go down the aisle. Unless you want a wedding, all it takes is a marriage license and a trip to city hall to get married. As a retired wedding coordinator, I don't see any reason that a wedding takes longer than eighteen months to execute. So, if you have accepted the role of "forever fiancée," you have settled for something less than what you want all because you've been with him so long that you're afraid to lose your investment.

One of my associates told me about her forty-something year old brother having been in an intimate relationship with a woman he lived with for years. He alleged that she had a problem managing money, which concerned him, and there had been many arguments between them about this. Apparently, she was of the mentality that this issue wasn't a big deal, especially when he stopped speaking about it with her. Less than a year after he dropped the issue, he packed his things and stayed with a family member while people were receiving invitations to his wedding in the mail. His wedding to someone else. When my associate asked her brother where the soon-to-be bride came from, he told her that he'd met her less than a year earlier, dated her, enjoyed her company, respected her, and left his prior situation once he determined that he wanted to wed her. In the meantime, the woman that he had spent years with pleaded her case to him, his family members, and anyone else that would listen, to no avail. She seemingly assumed that the time she put into their relationship overrode anything else and that she would be his bride one day. He proved her wrong.

My associate's brother never promised to marry the woman he'd spent over a decade with and, when he got tired of a habit that was an issue to him, he was free to walk away from her and did just that. I'm not taking sides; this situation is an example of time spent being of no consequence to a man when he is unhappy and wants to change his circumstances. My associate's brother was obviously ready for marriage. Even after all the years he spent with the first woman, he chose to become the husband of someone else with whom he'd spent way less time.

TRUTH #5:

A man can be with you for a vicennial, reap the benefits of your care, concern, love, money, body, and everything you have to give short of your health insurance, and still not get any closer to the altar than attending someone else's wedding.

Whatever you choose, the ultimate decision is yours. If you decide to waste even more time with a relationship that isn't providing you with what you want, you aren't securing your investment; you're "throwing good money after bad." You spent time with a man that is not giving you what you want and now you're doubling down because of the time you already committed? Come on, Ladies! All you're doing is subjecting yourselves to another month, another year, or another decade of unfulfilled dreams.

TAKEAWAY

1. How long is too long to wait for marriage? If you are with the right man and he professes to love, honor, and cherish you, then after conversations about what the marriage will look like (bills, children, housing, etc.) plus some premarital counseling by a licensed professional to make sure all of your bases are covered, you should be planning a trip to the courthouse or altar. I'm not suggesting six months is enough time, but a few years consisting of open and honest dialogue should be enough to either get married to or get free from this man.

2. Do not let your emotions blind you to the truth. If a man says that he does not see marriage in his future and that's what you see in yours, that should be a reason to stop the relationship from proceeding any further regardless of how much you like him.

3. Do not get mad at a man for standing on his word. If he told you up front that he was not the marrying type and you thought your

Lie #5

beauty, love for him, and your Platinum Pussy Package were enough to change his mind, that is not on him. That is on you.

4. Please don't tell me that you're still engaged to dude after five years! *Girl, Bye!* Seriously, if your goal is not to be a forever fiancée, don't allow yourself to become one. There are men that will keep you in the engagement phase forever because you let them. Do not bully or badger a man into marrying you. Either he wants you to be his wife or he does not. If, after a few conversations discussing the wedding and marriage, he isn't moving forward willingly, it's time you consider moving forward willingly . . . without him.

LIE #6

THE TWO OF US HAVE A BABY, SO HE'S GOING TO STAY WITH ME

My mother is a member of the silent generation; she was born in 1940. She sometimes looks at life a little differently than I do. One of the topics about which she stands on her blinged out soapbox is women having babies with men to whom they aren't married. Her issue is that some of the women think that having a man's baby will automatically grant them a lifelong pass to be a part of his life, but it does not. This is one of the topics about which she and I agree. I'm not swinging on single women having a baby. I was an unwed mother. When my son was born, I was plotting my escape from that relationship, so I had no intention or desire to stay in my son's father's life. (But that's another conversation.)

Because I'm in a different time in my life and most of my friends are grandmothers now, I don't hear this comment as much, but I remember overhearing "she's just trying to trap him" quite often when I was in my teens and twenties. That phrase referred to some young ladies who had children with men who hadn't or didn't marry them, and it was said by both the women who were my mom and aunt's ages as well as some of my acquaintances. It was assumed that, because of all the available forms of birth control at that time, if a woman conceived, she most likely wanted to be pregnant. And if she wasn't married, she did so to force the man's hand. In my mom's day and prior to that, there were more than a few "shotgun weddings," where young people were forced to get married because of an unplanned pregnancy.

The image of the shotgun wedding is that of a young woman who's expecting a baby standing in front of a minister next to a young man while her father has a shotgun to the young man's back. Her father is ensuring that the young man lives up to his obligations to the young lady and the baby while at the same time letting him know that the soon-to-be mother's reputation will not be sullied by his dalliance.

Lie #6

I don't know how those marriages turned out, but society has stepped away from that practice, leaving a lot of pregnant women husbandless.

Some women think that when a man has sex with you he loves you and a baby makes that love more solidified. But, for most men, sex is a physical release and has nothing to do with a declaration of their love for you. That's why a man can have multiple sex partners and not be emotionally connected to any of them. Having a baby doesn't change his feelings if he didn't already love you. Depending on what he thinks of you, a man may not even believe the baby you're having is his. That means he's either relegated you to the category of "everybody's semen receptacle" and has zero respect for you or he truly doesn't want to be in a relationship with you and will say any hurtful thing to let you know that.

Having encountered more than a few women that had children out of wedlock, some women complained that their children's fathers "weren't there for us." When I inquired about exactly who "us" was, I was told that he should be there for the women and the babies. My asking them about the rationality of their expecting a man to "be there" for a woman with which he wasn't in a relationship was met with blank stares. I one hundred percent advocate for both parents supporting their children on all levels—mental, emotional, physical, financial, and spiritual. But how does that translate to your child's father being there for you?

He should want you to be safe, happy, and a plethora of wonderful things because your state of being affects his child. But he is not responsible for making you happy, keeping a roof over your head, putting food on your table, and all of the other things adults are responsible for doing for themselves. He's responsible for clothing, feeding, and attending to his children, but not you as their mother. You were going to have to do those things for yourself when you didn't have a child so why would you think that your child's father is responsible for doing those things for you now?

Your baby should not be used as your meal ticket or your way to attempt to guilt trip your child's father into being your financial sponsor. You should pay for the lifestyle you choose and he should help pay for the lifestyle of the child you share. Your hair, nails, and wardrobe are your responsibility. Your man can pay for these items also but, if your child's father is not your man, keeping you in diamonds and red bottoms is not his obligation or concern. Discuss the expenses for your child's wants and needs (schooling, clothes, sporting activities, etc.) with your child's father and work together to pay for those items. That is his duty as a father and yours as a mother.

TRUTH #6:

Having the baby does not mean you have the man. Having the baby makes him obligated to the baby. It does not make him obligated to you.

What was the conversation the two of you had when you discovered that you were pregnant? The expectations for both parties should have been discussed way before the baby's birth. If both of you have a compatible view of how you're going to proceed as a couple and as parents, that's awesome! If your view of the future includes being in a relationship and his does not, please figure out how you and he can both be amazing parents to the child without being a couple. The baby deserves two happy parents that make him or her their priority and have a partnership based on parenting if they're no longer intimate.

TAKEAWAY

1. Unless you are legally his wife, a man has no real responsibility for you even if you are his child's mother. You are responsible for you. The both of you are responsible for the child.

2. If you are no longer in an above-board relationship with your child's father, you have no say in who he dates or marries.

3. If you have feelings for your child's father that are not reciprocated, trust that there is a reason the two of you are no longer together. Work towards fulfilling your goals and improving yourself while letting that level of attachment to him dissipate.

4. Please don't tell me that you had that baby to try to keep that dude in your life. *Girl, Bye!* Seriously, do not expect that you being pregnant will change anything about the relationship between you and your child's father, unless he decides he wants something different or you choose something different

that is in your best interest and the best interest of your child.

LIE #7

HAVING HIS BABY GIVES ME A REAL TITLE WITH RIGHTS

"Baby mama" is a phrase I've heard almost every day for the past thirty years in conversation, in movies, and in songs. Depending on the person or situation, it's said with reverence, disdain, or even neutrality. Some women say it about themselves with pride. Some women say it as a put-down of another woman, especially if her man is the father of another woman's child. Some people are so used to the phrase that they use it with no emotional association one way or the other.

During the eras when most women were both wives and mothers, I don't think this phrase was used. I certainly didn't hear it when I was growing up. Now, with there being so many single mothers, some people seem to think that the term "baby mama" is a replacement for "wife and mother." It isn't.

Being a wife gives a woman legal standing and rights. You may have a fantastic relationship with your child's father and be invited to his family's functions, and that's great, but know that your child is related to them and a wife would be related to them through marriage . . . you are not.

An associate of mine has a daughter with a woman with whom he was previously in a relationship. The two of them broke up when their daughter was an infant but co-parented her so she would have the benefits of being raised by both parents. His daughter's mom was always welcome to attend his family's functions, even after their daughter got older. Everything appeared to be fine until my associate started seriously dating another woman and decided to propose to her. At his family functions, his daughter's mom started asserting her "position" as his baby mama and being beloved by his family in an apparent bid to either intimidate or humiliate his fiancée. His baby mama's level of disrespect for his fiancée reached such heights that the woman to which he was committed decided that this was not a situation in which she wanted to remain, so she broke off the engagement.

Putting my associate's culpability aside, why would any woman who is not in a relationship with a man but has a child with him feel that she has the right to operate like this? There are a few possible answers—she still has feelings for her child's father that are not being reciprocated, she's still in a sexual relationship with her child's father but that's all he's willing to offer her, she's only happy when he is single, or she does not want to be replaced by another woman in his family's affections. Maybe there's an answer I have not considered. Whatever the case, this woman isn't the only woman I've seen staring down their child's father's new girlfriend or heard of physically attacking her child's father's new love interest because, at the end of the day, she felt that being his baby mama gave her that right.

A woman I know met a man she really liked, and he liked her. They started dating and soon chose to be in a relationship. She didn't have any children, but he had one with a woman with whom he'd previously been in a relationship. Allegedly, the man still did everything that he had previously done for his child but was no longer available to the mother of the child. Out of respect for his new relationship, he decided to restrict his actions to those solely dealing with his offspring and no longer entertained the mother's wants and needs. His baby mama was upset because she wanted to re-establish the relationship she previously had with her child's father, but he was not interested and had moved on with his life. The couple decided to move in together and that, apparently, caused the baby mama to segue from just being perturbed to becoming violent. The child's mother decided to wait in the bushes for the girlfriend to return home and, when she did, the baby mama jumped out and physically assaulted the unsuspecting woman.

When you're willing to sit in the bushes, possibly for hours, and risk a prison sentence because your status as baby mama has been jeopardized, it's seriously time to introspect about your life and enlist a therapist to help you untangle your thought processes so you can regain your mental health.

TRUTH #7:

Doctor is a title. Esquire is a title. Mrs. is a title. Titles come with rights and privileges, from operating at certain hospitals to being the recipient of your husband's pension after his death. Being a baby mama is not a title and the only right it gives you is being your child's mother.

In today's world, we have gotten comfortable with giving titles to those not fulfilling the job description and we often confuse which titles match which jobs. For example, when you give someone the title "my man," do you have a description of what that title means to you so you can convey those details to him and see if he wants to step into that role? Conversely, be clear that being a baby mama means just that—you are the mother of his child. It does not grant you lifelong access to the child's father nor does it obligate him to *you*; his responsibility is to his child. You do not have the right to attend his family's functions or to be a disruptive force in his life. Even though your intimate relationship has ended, the title both of you should aspire to have is awesome parent. You can be spectacular co-parents without having another level of connection.

Lie #7

TAKEAWAY

1. Being someone's baby mama comes with no rights and is not a relevant title except to your child.
2. If your relationship with your child's father does not work out, being a co-parent is an honorable achievement!
3. The new woman in your child's father's life can be an ally instead of an enemy. Get to know her as she will spend time with your child, and it makes sense to know what type of person she is and how she feels about your precious little (or big) one.
4. Please don't tell me that you're waiting in the bushes or anywhere else to confront the woman that is currently dating your child's father. *Girl, Bye!* Seriously, if you are so enmeshed with what might have been and you think that she's the reason you are not with this man, you're wrong. That man made his decision, not the new woman. Respect his choice and keep loving your life. He is not worth you dishonoring your name and

possible incarceration because you let your misplaced emotions get the best of you.

HE DIDN'T MEAN IT

Here in Lie #8, I will address two specific reasons that women accept the excuse, "I didn't mean it." There may be more times that this lie is deployed, but I'm only dealing with the most frequent cases in which I've heard this rationale used. These cases are also the most damaging mentally, physically, and emotionally.

Cheating

If you are dating a man and have had the conversation that defines your relationship as one of fidelity, you expect that man, your man, to be monogamous. If you ever find out that he's been unfaithful to you, I'm sure that he gave you a reason.

"I was drunk" is a good one. It takes the responsibility off the man and places it on the liquor. But, if a man knows that his inhibitions are lower when he drinks, why would he consume the alcohol somewhere that he was vulnerable to having sex outside of his relationship? Somewhere you weren't present? How many of us have been at a club and been propositioned by an intoxicated dude wearing the biggest wedding ring ever, talking about how he "saw your gorgeous legs from across the room and wondered if you'd give him the chance to get between them." If you asked about the wedding band, I promise that the standard answer was "I'm almost divorced." Boy, bye! This excuse is garbage.

"She seduced me" is just pitiful. A grown man is in total control of his body. Even if someone is holding a gun to his head, he still chooses how he's going to react. As Bell Biv DeVoe said in their song "Poison," "you can't trust a big butt and a smile." So, if a man knows a big butt is his weakness and he also knows that he's dedicated himself to you, it's up to him to stay away from situations where there are big butts that don't belong to you and space for sex to happen. The husband of one of my friend's was asked by a female church member to repair something at her home. My friend was at work plus she knew the woman, so she didn't think she needed to accompany him. When the church member called my friend to brag about how she'd slept with her husband and was going to marry him, my friend was astonished. Her husband's only answer was, "I fixed her computer, she made me lunch, and we were just talking when she opened her robe and seduced me." So, he went from a tuna sandwich to the real fish between the church lady's legs. GTFOH! The moment she came to the door in her robe, he knew what time it was and, instead of leaving, he got paid for fixing a computer with a Pussy Package. (I don't know if hers was Platinum.)

"It didn't mean anything" is so demeaning in that he thinks that he can tell you anything. If it didn't mean anything, why did he do it? Even the sister statement of this reason, "she didn't mean anything," is ludicrous. How did he luck up on a woman with whom he had sex, but he has the luxury of relegating her to the status of being totally irrelevant? Yes, he may have just used her as a semen receptacle but she's relevant as she's the person with whom he chose to risk his relationship with you. I was living with a man that didn't know how resourceful I am when I know someone is lying to me. When the reasons he gave for being out at certain times, not being where he claimed he would be, and a plethora of other excuses just didn't add up, I politely looked in spaces that I typically never touched and *voila*! There were the letters from his paramour. When I confronted him with the evidence, all he could say was, "she didn't mean anything." After I cussed him all the way out (I used to be the Queen of Cursing), I started working on my exit strategy. Beyond the hurt because of the infidelity, his insulting my intelligence with this weak justification made me despise him even more.

If he believed the next excuse, "every man cheats anyway," then why didn't he admit to this philosophy initially so you'd know he was going to be a serial adulterer? I met a guy who had just gotten divorced from his wife of fifteen years with whom he had four children. When I asked him why they were divorced, he was brutally honest. He traveled to certain cities for his job and had a woman in every one of them. Everything was cool (for him) until his wife found out and, after his behavior didn't change, got tired of his shenanigans and found herself a side piece too. My associate was so outdone that he filed for the divorce! He said that he still loved his wife but couldn't get past her cheating on him. Incredulous, I reiterated what he'd told me to be sure I understood—he had multiple women over an extended amount of time, had promised to stop cheating on his wife, didn't stop cheating, and asked for a divorce when she stepped out on him. He confirmed that I heard him correctly but "every man cheats, so that shouldn't have made her cheat on him." You could have knocked me over with a feather! I asked him if he had expressed this philosophy to her prior to marrying her and he told me he had not because "everybody knows that." He's the first person I gave the title "serial adulterer."

"I have a high sex drive and you don't want to have sex enough" or "you don't want to have sex the way I like it" should have been discussed before the man found his way into another woman's vagina. Some men have a high libido and would like to have sex a couple of times a day. If a man with high sexual urges is in a relationship with a woman that has a much lower sexual appetite, this can be a problem. The man will be frustrated because his needs aren't being met and the woman will be unhappy because she's being pressured into accommodating his desire for sex. There are some people that are more sexually adventurous than others. If he wants to have sex outside where the neighbors may see, in an airplane washroom, or on the dining room table and you aren't willing to take your lovemaking outside of the four walls of your bedroom, you're going to have conflict. If doggy style, teabagging, or reverse cowgirl are high on his list of sex acts and you're only comfortable with missionary, Houston, we have a problem.

I'm not saying that you're wrong for your choices about your sex life. But, if you aren't willing or able to have sex with the frequency and in the locations and positions he'd like, and he isn't willing or able to modify his urges, then you aren't sexually compatible. Sexual incompatibility is going to be an ongoing issue, so unless there's a middle ground where the two of you can meet, this may not be the best relationship for either of you.

Here's my all-time favorite, "It just happened!" I am waiting for the day that someone can explain how a man can be out one day, minding his business, and he just happened to luck up on an exposed vagina and his penis became unsheathed with no assistance and just fell into someone's lady parts. When a man has sex with you without wearing a condom and soon you start to feel itchy and uncomfortable in your private region and—knowing you have not been with anyone else sexually or changed your laundry detergent or body wash—you go to your physician who confirms that you have a sexually transmitted infection (STI), don't be the queen of self-deception; not only did he cheat on you, he did so in a manner that didn't protect you or himself. Don't allow him to tell you that he didn't mean to give you herpes, gonorrhea, or any of the list of sexually transmitted diseases. His actions clearly show that he meant to have unprotected sex and didn't care about the potential consequences for either of you.

If you poll women, most will agree that cheating is not solely a physical act. Although I firmly believe that men and women can have platonic relationships, there are those who use the term "friendship" to cover up the true nature of the liaison, which is an emotional relationship. When you establish any kind of connection with someone and choose to develop a relationship with that person, you are operating with intent. If a man is in a friendship with a woman and that's all it is, he intended for that connection to only be a friendship. If a man is in a relationship with you but is operating emotionally with another woman in a manner similar to the way he does with you, it may be time for you to have a conversation with him about the parameters of his association with that woman.

If your intuition tells you that his "work wife" (a term I have a problem with) wants to be more than just friends or he enjoys the woman's fawning over him or whatever you see that indicates to you that their union is too close for your comfort, communicate your feelings to him and assess his response as well as his or their actions. Even without sex being involved, I don't know many women that want their man or husband to be another woman's emotional support system.

Lie #8

Abuse

At my previous place of employment, I worked at the area's domestic violence courthouse. There were many different types of abusers, and they crossed all gender, age, ethnicity, and socio-economic demographics. The relationships between those that were abusers and the abused were siblings, parents and children, roommates, and extended biological familial relationships such as cousins or aunts. But the overwhelming majority of relationships that fell under this umbrella were intimate partner relationships.

Of the intimate partnerships, there were same sex relationships as well as heterosexual relationships. The vast majority of intimate partner relationships where domestic violence became a legal issue were between a man (who was the perpetrator) and a woman (who was the victim). For the purposes of this book, the offenders are men, and the victims are women.

So many people experience domestic violence on levels that are not physical. Domestic violence can be verbal abuse, sexual violence, psychological abuse, and economic abuse as well. Physical violence includes, but is not limited to, beating, kicking, punching, biting, spitting, burning, choking, and using objects such as ropes, knives, and guns. Verbal abuse can be public or private demeaning, cursing, and threatening the victim, people she loves, or things she loves (like pets). I cannot tell you how many women I know that have children and have been told, "no one else will want you with all these kids so you aren't going anywhere." Or the infamous, "who do you think wants your fat/ugly/stupid ass but me?" Non-consensual sexual contact where the abuser uses his body parts (penis, tongue, fingers, etc.) or an object (like a broom handle) to penetrate any orifice of the victim as well as marital rape, forced pregnancies, and forced abortions are examples of sexual violence.

Women endure this assault because they don't want this abuse to become more extreme. Two examples of psychological abuse are threatening behavior (like punching walls) and forcibly isolating the victim. Even though he hasn't hit her, he is letting her know that he will really hurt her if and when he decides to punch her in the face. If she has no contact with her family and friends, they aren't able to help her plan her getaway. When an offender engages in economic abuse, he can take away the victim's earning potential by not allowing her to go to work, or he can take her earnings from her and restrict her movements so she misses days at work which reflects poorly on her employment record. Without money, she cannot finance her escape and he knows that.

Most of the domestic violence I saw at work was physical. Some of the women would become regulars at the courthouse because the incidents of domestic violence happened on a frequent basis. A lot of times, the women were not the ones that called the police; their children and neighbors called 911. Sadly, it takes quite a few incidents of domestic violence for most victims to personally call for help. Because she usually just wants the attack to stop at that moment, it takes even more time and incidents of violence to occur before she is willing to appear in court and testify against her abuser. Some women (despite the severity of their injuries, their children being a witness to the person that is supposed to love their mom being the one to hurt her the most, or their loss of employment and other consequences) choose to stay with their abusers.

"He didn't mean it" is one of the top reasons given when victims were asked why they were going to stay in those harrowing environments. Some victims minimize the violence inflicted upon them and sincerely believe that "he's going to change this time." I am not victim blaming; there is a lot involved with the psyche of a woman that is living in a household where domestic violence is prevalent. If you ask the perpetrators of the violence, a lot of them give the same responses as their victims: "I'm going to change," "I didn't mean it," or they blame alcohol and being drunk for their behavior. Some men blame the victim and justify punching her in the face because she said or did something not to his liking.

TRUTH #8:

A man that hurts you and dishonors you *meant* to do just that. He *chose* to degrade you and there is no excuse for him treating you that way.

Lie #8

Whether a man decides to cheat on you physically, get involved with another woman emotionally, or assaults you violently, his behavior is not due to the fact that he cannot control himself. His decision to disrespect or injure you is a choice. If he is unhappy with your relationship, he is free to discontinue it at any time instead of demeaning you, harming you, or potentially killing you. Unless there is a mental health condition that renders him unable to control his mind, a grown man has full, complete jurisdiction over his behaviors and operates as he chooses.

TAKEAWAY

1. You must love yourself enough to set the boundaries for what is acceptable versus unacceptable treatment. Short of rape and murder, most people treat you the way you allow them to treat you. Once you see the abusive tendencies, get away from that person as if your life depends on it because your life actually does depend on it.

2. If you're in an abusive situation and are having difficulty detaching from the abuser, call the domestic abuse hotlines for referrals and support. Get to a safe space that most of your circle doesn't know about. (Too often, family and friends will tell the abuser about the victim's whereabouts.) Then, engage a therapist that will help you unearth the reasons you chose to stay. Make a plan to rebuild your life and stay on your new journey free of the encumbrances of disrespect, abuse, and shame. Be extremely careful as the majority of domestic violence victims are killed attempting to leave the situation or after the relationship has ended.

3. Infidelity can be physical as well as emotional. A man that has sex with another woman or is the emotional support system (beyond platonic friendship) for another woman is dishonoring you and your relationship with him.

4. Please don't tell me that you're taking another round of antibiotics because that dude slept with the Dirty McNasty chick yet again and gave you the itchy scratchy yet again! *Girl, Bye!* Seriously, a man that has a physical or emotional connection with another woman saw it coming and did nothing to prevent it or to protect you from it. He had a choice and he made it. He did not choose you.

IF I LOVE HIM ENOUGH, HE WILL CHANGE

None of us likes everything about another person. If we're totally honest, none of us is in love with everything about ourselves. One question to ask yourself regarding someone else is, "What percentage of the traits I see in this person do I like?" Another question is, "Am I able to accept the traits that I don't like?" There may be things that a person can say or do that will irritate you, even if you love him. Something small to one person, like someone cracking his knuckles, may be a trigger for someone else and is intolerable.

Whatever the vice or the behavior is, there's a reason someone does it. A person may crack his or her knuckles because that action relieves the tightness in the joints, or it may be a subconscious response to being nervous. It's good to know why a person does the things you like as well as the things you don't instead of assuming you know the reason.

In an intimate relationship, it's extremely important to know what drives a man's behavior because, if you plan to spend the rest of your life with him, knowing the reason behind his thoughts and deeds is major. If there is something he says or does that is troubling to you, it can be a problem that is at the red flag level. Bring that action to his attention in a non-confrontational conversation so he can disclose his reasons for doing it and discuss if it is something he can or wants to decrease in frequency or stop altogether. Some behaviors are so ingrained, he may not even recognize what he's doing.

Be aware that you do not have the power to change a man without using extreme force, and sometimes even that isn't successful. You cannot love a man so much that he stops doing what you dislike or starts doing what you want. You can cry, scream, withhold sex, have more sex, use all kinds of methods, yet you still will not make him change. Your love and acts of persuasion will temporarily bring about a couple of changes, but real change, yours and his, comes from within.

TRUTH #9:

His love for you will cause him to change, not *your* love for him. That and, depending on the situation, therapy. Some people won't change for Jesus.

As women, we sometimes think that our love is enough to make a crooked line straight. The reality is that you cannot love a man to the point that he will stop his thoughts and behaviors that are hurtful to you. If change is to be long-lasting, it originates from within. So, if there is something in a man that he wants to change, he will do so because he decides to live differently. He will make those adjustments because he values you and cherishes your relationship so much that he will walk through flames wearing gasoline-soaked briefs to maintain his life with you. He will do it because he loves you.

TAKEAWAY

1. Identify the behaviors that are problematic and discuss them with your partner. If he agrees with your assessment, talk about his method for instituting the changes. Some issues are serious enough to merit counseling and there is no shame in that.

2. If he keeps telling you that he's trying but you see no noticeable progress, reiterate your concerns and, if he's willing, map out a new plan of action. If he still operates in the same manner, then you have a decision to make.

3. If there is a roadblock preventing him from making the changes that he agrees are necessary, enlist a counselor or therapist for individual and couples counseling. Find out the real reason he cannot commit to the behaviors that will improve your relationship.

4. Please don't tell me that you're still talking to him about the same issues you had ten years ago! *Girl, Bye!* Seriously, if a man loves you

enough, he will change for the better, not only because you asked him to but because he wants to be a better man, husband, lover, provider, and friend for and to you.

IT'S OKAY TO BE CALLED A BITCH

Per Dictionary.com, the noun bitch means "a female dog; a female canine generally; a malicious, unpleasant, selfish person, especially a woman." Other uses are "a lewd woman; disparaging and offensive; any woman; a person, especially a woman (often used as a term of address): 'Hey bitches, let's go party!'"

The times I've heard men refer to women in which they're in a relationship in this way are more numerous than I care to remember. "That's my bottom bitch" is a phrase that pimps used to identify the prostitute that had been a part of his stable of women the longest and made the most money for him. Now, random dudes that are playing at pimping say this about the women that bond them out of jail (or visit them while in custody and make sure there is money on their books), buy them gifts and video games, and fight the other women that buddy deals with on his command. Sadly, these ladies seem to think that being a bottom bitch is a compliment, not understanding that a man who calls you a bitch has absolutely no respect for you and figures that you don't have any respect for yourself.

I was raised in an environment and by a family that dictated you fought if someone called you a bitch because that person's intent was to humiliate and disrespect you by calling you a female dog. If anyone called me a bitch, I was supposed to beat the brakes off them. I don't know when the informal use came into vogue and have definitely heard "bitch" being used in a way that was not intended to be malicious in recent years. I still have trouble with that.

Having worked in the criminal justice system for quite a while, every now and then somebody lost their mind and called me a bitch. Initially, I had to think about losing my job, being arrested and charged with attempted murder (because I would be trying to commit a homicide), and my son not having another parent to keep me from punching that person in the mouth. Later, I understood the anger that person expressed wasn't really about me, it was about the criminal justice system for which I was a representative. (I still wasn't okay with them calling me a bitch, but I extended them some grace and let it go.)

Regardless of the gender of the person hurling the insult, the intent is typically the same—to offend, degrade, and disrespect you. In my life, I've been called a bitch by women way more than men (at least to my face) which I find to be sad. In my mind, the woman calling me a bitch is not only seeking to hurt me, but someone in her world has most likely called her a bitch so much and made her feel so low about herself that she spews that verbal vomit onto another woman.

She thinks so little of herself that she wants to tear down any woman that holds herself in high regard, so she won't be alone in that dark place of her abused soul. The men that have called me a bitch seemed to think that I needed to be brought down a notch or two. What they didn't know is they didn't have the power to reduce my status or my soul. Nor did they know that I had no problem talking about them, or their mamas for giving birth to them, and I wasn't afraid to fight. I am much nicer now but please don't try me.

The logic some people use is that claiming a word as your own diffuses its initial intent and negative connotations. I understand this perspective, but I disagree with it. All that does is give the others that are using the word by its original definition another reason to justify dishonoring you. If you call yourself a bitch, then they feel that it's certainly fine for them to call you a bitch and mean all the disrespect the word conveys.

TRUTH #10:

The word bitch is a derogatory term when directed at or used to describe a woman. Period.

Lie #10

TAKEAWAY

1. A bitch is a female dog, or a negative, demeaning term used to disrespect women.

2. A man that calls you a bitch thinks you are less than garbage.

3. A woman that calls you a bitch wants you to think that you're less than garbage and just may see herself in the same light.

4. "Bitch, I was just playing with you. You be tripping." *Girl, Bye!* Seriously, be mindful of how you let people address you. I'd hate for you to find out that while you thought that person was playing with you, he or she really feels you're a bitch in the worst way possible.

CONCLUSION

This book was not written from a place of judgment. I've walked through some of these fires personally and observed people, some of them being friends I care about, endure the rest. If you see yourself engaging in any of these lies and have some difficulty getting to your truth, I encourage you to seek council—a friend, an elder, or a therapist. Start your journey to self-help, self-love, peace, and recovery.

Change is hard, even when we know we need to make transitions within ourselves and in our lives. Do not be ashamed if you need to seek counseling. When I couldn't make sense of how my life was spiraling out of control, I saw a licensed therapist. She helped me uncover some fears I wasn't consciously aware that I had, which allowed me to work through them and adjust my thought patterns. Getting to the root of the reasons you've made certain choices will help you understand your subconscious motivations better. Knowing what has driven you to think and act in particular ways in the past allows you the freedom to make different decisions now.

I don't care who you are or what you've done; you can start anew today. Be the woman you always dreamed of! Be the woman you'd like your daughter to emulate and become! Be the woman that makes her ancestors and herself proud! That woman is already in you. You are a beautiful, compassionate, intelligent, talented, classy, and wonderfully amazing woman! Look in the mirror and see your radiance, beauty, and power. Then, step outside and let the world see you shine!

ACKNOWLEDGMENTS

There have been so many people that supported my decision to write this book. Pam Braxton, my best friend who always reels me in when I've jumped in water that is too deep. Sherri Jordan, whose support is immeasurable. Marcia Hawthorne, who offered her help in any way I needed it. LaTanya Mitchell, who shook her head as she got on board. And, Tequila Lucas, who always makes sure as best she can that my presentation is proper.

I also want to acknowledge all the ladies that have had *Girl, Bye!* moments and lived to tell the tale. Because of your courage, transparency, and honesty, there are daughters, friends, associates, and family members that have had the chance to learn from your mistakes. You saved them from having to go down those dark paths themselves. Now, after bearing witness to your growth and elevation, they get to celebrate your positive transformation. Thank you!

ABOUT THE AUTHOR

Ria Rai Harris is the CEO of Dusk 2 Daybreak Transformational Coaching and Speaking International, founder and national director of the Beyond Beautiful World Pageant, and a licensed realtor in Illinois, Indiana, and Punta Cana.

Born and raised on the south side of Chicago, Ria earned her bachelor of science in psychology and rhetoric from the University of Illinois Urbana-Champaign. She is a life member of Sigma Gamma Rho Sorority, Incorporated.

Challenging women to overcome the fear of success in their careers, relationships, and lives is her primary mission. She also enjoys reading, archery, listening to music, and engaging in discussions about topics that interest her in order to gain a better understanding of others' thoughts.

Ria currently resides in Chicago, Illinois. She has been married to her husband, Daniel Yarbough, since 2016. She has one son, A. Ahmad Hill, and her trusty sidekick, Black the Wonder Dog.

Learn more at
www.riaraispeaks.com

CREATING DISTINCTIVE BOOKS WITH INTENTIONAL RESULTS

We're a collaborative group of creative masterminds with a mission to produce high-quality books to position you for monumental success in the marketplace.

Our professional team of writers, editors, designers, and marketing strategists work closely together to ensure that every detail of your book is a clear representation of the message in your writing.

Want to know more?
Write to us at info@publishyourgift.com
or call (888) 949-6228

Discover great books, exclusive offers, and more at
www.PublishYourGift.com

Connect with us on social media

@publishyourgift

www.ingramcontent.com/pod-product-compliance
Lightning Source LLC
Chambersburg PA
CBHW071901070526
44583CB00016B/1797